T0402871

GOING WILD

Animals in Nature

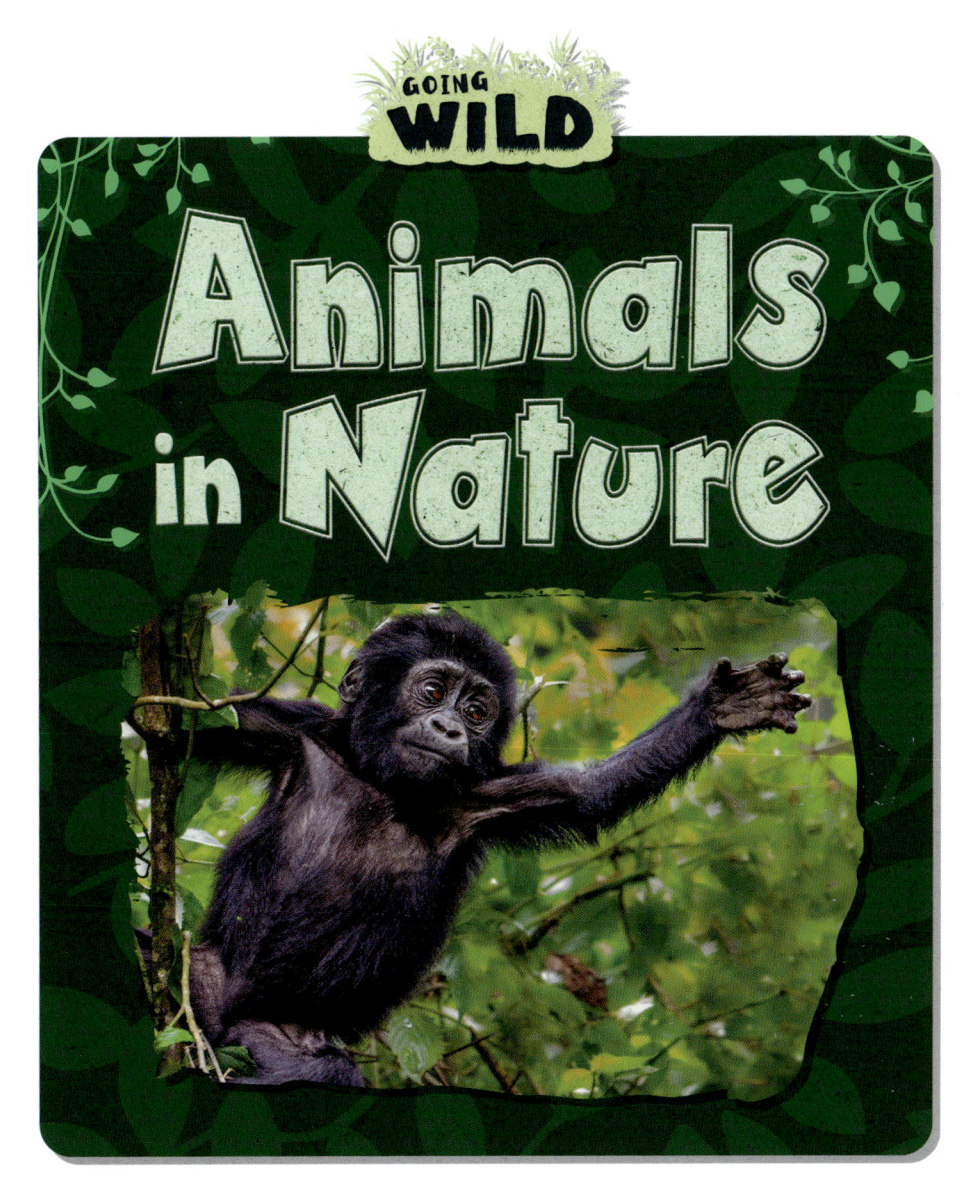

by Noah Leatherland

BEARPORT
PUBLISHING

Minneapolis, Minnesota

Credits
All images courtesy of Shutterstock. With thanks to Getty Images, Thinkstock Photo, and iStockphoto. Recurring images – Very_Very, Barbara.M.Mattson, Apostrophe, ArtKio, Ton Photographer 4289. Cover – CNuisin, Digital Draw Studio, Malenkka, Mazhar Rind. 2–3 – Yantar. 4–5 – ArtMediaFactory, Damsea, Nazzu, Zdan Ivan. 6–7 – Anan Kaewkhammul, Andrei Armiagov, Jay Ondreicka, TommoT. 8–9 – Oriol Querol, Michaela Pilch, GizmoPhoto, Michael Fitzsimmons. 10–11 – Favious, Panga Media, Rich Carey, Danny Ye. 12–13 – Tom Jastram, kennyc, Maggy Meyer, Emma Geary. 14–15 – Jedsada Naeprai, Svitlana Kazachek, Mikai, boyphare. 16–17 – JonShore, Kaentian Street, Rich Carey, VanderWolf Images, Mary Terriberry. 18–19 – WIJI, Photo Spirit, FloridaStock, Christian Roberts-Olsen, Flystock. 20–21 – VIKVAD, Karel Cerny, Jacob Lund, casa.da.photo. 22–23 – GUDKOV ANDREY, Rich4-max, Nikolai Denisov, Louis Imbeau, CC BY 4.0 via Wikimedia Commons. 24–25 – Erni, Yantar, Chris Ison, Blue Planet Studio, Jason Benz Bennee. 26–27 – Sunti, VE.Studio, tawanroong, VesnaArt. 28–29 – POP-THAILAND, L. Feddes, Avigator Fortuner, Luoxi, Ancha Chiangmai. 30–31 – Piu_Piu, Jeroen Mikkers.

Bearport Publishing Company Product Development Team
President: Jen Jenson; Director of Product Development: Spencer Brinker; Managing Editor: Allison Juda; Associate Editor: Naomi Reich; Associate Editor: Tiana Tran; Art Director: Colin O'Dea; Designer: Kim Jones; Designer: Kayla Eggert; Product Development Assistant: Owen Hamlin

Library of Congress Cataloging-in-Publication Data is available at www.loc.gov or upon request from the publisher.

ISBN: 979-8-88916-976-5 (hardcover)
ISBN: 979-8-89232-153-2 (ebook)

© 2025 BookLife Publishing
This edition is published by arrangement with BookLife Publishing.

North American adaptations © 2025 Bearport Publishing Company. All rights reserved. No part of this publication may be reproduced in whole or in part, stored in any retrieval system, or transmitted in any form or by any means, electronic, mechanical, photocopying, recording, or otherwise, without written permission from the publisher. Bearport Publishing is a division of Chrysalis Education Group.

For more information, write to Bearport Publishing, 5357 Penn Avenue South, Minneapolis, MN 55419.

CONTENTS

GOING WILD

Earth is home to many different animals swimming in the sea, flying in the sky, and wandering over the land. Together with plants, these animals form communities of interconnected life all around the planet.

These communities are called **ecosystems**. Each ecosystem has a landscape and **climate** that support the lives of the plants and animals living in it.

Common squirrel monkeys

Often, plants need a certain **climate** to grow. These plants become food for some animals that, in turn, become food for meat-eating animals. In this way, all life in an ecosystem is connected.

All animals, big and small, play an important role in their ecosystems.

Humans are animals, too! They live in ecosystems with other living things. Unfortunately, some human actions can damage these shared homes and harm their animal neighbors.

5

ANIMALS NEED OUR HELP

Cutting down just one tree can affect the lives of many animals.

All over the planet, human actions have put animals in danger. We pollute the air and water. Humans have cut down forests to build homes and businesses. Animals cannot undo the damage we have done, so we need to help them however we can.

Sometimes, humans completely destroy animal homes to make space for their own.

When humans damage one part of an ecosystem through pollution or **deforestation**, other parts of the same ecosystem may also be harmed.

However, helping one part of an ecosystem can also help other parts. Each animal in an ecosystem helps support the lives of other animals. If we find ways to protect the most endangered animals in an ecosystem, the entire community will be healthier.

By helping animals, humans create a healthier world for all living things. If we don't help the animals we share the world with, there is a risk that some of them could disappear forever.

The white rhino has come close to becoming **extinct**.

7

ENDANGERED AND EXTINCT

Some animals have been harmed by changes to their ecosystems more than others. They have seen their homes and food supplies shrink or disappear. These changes can threaten their lives. Animals are said to be endangered when they are at risk of dying off completely.

Asian elephants were declared endangered in 1986.

Western chimpanzee

WESTERN CHIMPANZEE

In recent years, the number of Western chimpanzees dropped by 80 percent. That means that more than three out of every four western chimps have disappeared. Experts believe their **population** will continue to shrink if we don't act fast.

Animals are extinct when there are none left alive on the planet. Some animals can be found only in **captivity**, which means they are extinct in the wild.

The scimitar oryx was declared extinct in the wild in 2000.

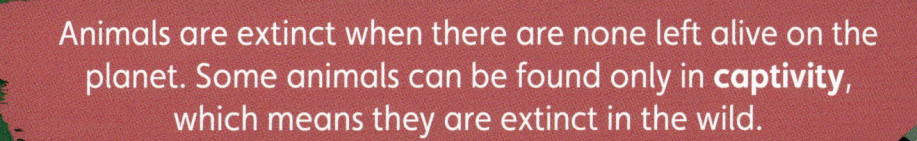

Guam kingfisher

GUAM KINGFISHER

The Guam kingfisher was a bird found only on the island of Guam. However, in the 1980s, it became extinct in the wild. Today, there are only about 140 living in captivity.

The loss of one animal in an ecosystem can harm the other animals they lived with and supported.

9

DEFORESTATION

Thousands of trees have been cut down in this forest.

Deforestation, or the cutting down of trees, is one of the human activities that harms animals. It destroys their homes and often removes major sources of food and water.

People cut down trees for wood and to clear space for buildings and farms. However, many animals make their homes in and around trees. Without somewhere to live, animal populations die or are forced to **migrate**.

SPIX'S MACAW

Spix's macaw is a blue bird that lived in the dry forests of Caatinga in Brazil. Unfortunately, many of the trees there have been cut down to make space for farmland.

Spix's macaw

The last time a Spix's macaw was seen in the wild was in 2000. Today, there are fewer than 200 of these birds living in captivity.

HUNTERS AND POACHERS

NATURE·RESERVE

Humans have hunted animals for thousands of years. People hunt for food, to protect farms from **predators**, and to stop some animal populations from getting too big.

Some animals that are at risk are protected from hunters by law. However, there are still people who kill these animals. This is called poaching. Poachers usually sell parts of the animal's body, such as its horns or fur.

Rangers work to stop poachers.

BLACK RHINO

Black rhinos live across the southern and eastern parts of Africa. It is estimated that there were nearly one million of the animals in 1900. Since then, hunters and poachers have brought black rhinos close to extinction.

Black rhinos are poached for their horns.

By 1995, illegal poaching had made the black rhino population drop to fewer than 2,500 in the wild.

POLLUTION

Litter is a type of pollution.

When humans burn fuel to power cars, factories, and homes, they make **toxic** pollution. Humans also produce deadly waste as they create some kinds of plastics and metals.

Pollution can make some animal **habitats** unlivable. It can even poison and kill some animals.

Lots of waste ends up being dumped in wilderness areas.

SOIL POLLUTION

Toxic waste can be invisible. However, the ground beneath your feet may still be polluted.

An oil spill leaking into soil

There are lots of **chemicals** that farmers put on their fields to grow bigger and better crops or to keep away insects. But these chemicals are often poisonous to nearby animals.

Pesticides are chemicals used to protect crops from insects.

The soil can also be polluted when waste is not disposed of properly. Waste from landfills, mines, and factories can leak into the soil. This harms an ecosystem's plants and the animals that rely on them for food and shelter.

WATER POLLUTION

Lakes, rivers, and oceans around the world have been polluted by human waste products.

During a rainfall, chemicals from farmlands get washed into streams. Waste water from sewers and factories can be treated to remove some harmful chemicals, but a lot of toxins still get into rivers and oceans. Poisonous chemicals entering the water can severely damage habitats and kill wildlife.

Trash in the ocean is very dangerous to wildlife. It can be deadly for animals that get tangled in it. Some animals die when they eat the trash.

AIR POLLUTION

Even the air can be polluted by humans. Some cars, trucks, and planes run on **fossil fuels**. When burned, fossil fuels release a gas called carbon dioxide that pollutes the air. Factories and power plants also let out carbon dioxide and other poisonous chemicals.

Polluted air can harm or kill animals that breathe it in. It can also harm the plants that animals eat. When rain falls through polluted air, it can become what's known as acid rain. This poisons the soil and kills the plants and trees that grow in it.

Acid rain can seriously damage plants.

CLIMATE CHANGE

Climate change is making some places much hotter and drier.

Climate is the usual weather of a place, including its rainfall and temperature. Earth's climate has naturally changed for millions of years. Recently, however, humans have made changes happen much faster.

Animals rely on normal shifts in weather and the seasons to let them know when it is time to migrate, seek shelter, have babies, and look for certain kinds of food. But climate change is disrupting normal animal behavior and making it harder for them to survive.

Swallows migrate during the cold weather of winter months.

Changing temperatures makes some areas too hot or too cold for animals to survive. Polar ice is melting because of rising temperatures, destroying the homes of arctic animals, such as polar bears.

In parts of the world where it is getting hotter and drier, deadly wildfires can destroy entire ecosystems. Climate change is also making the oceans warmer. Warmer water damages some ocean habitats, such as the coral reefs that support and shelter thousands of **species** of sea creatures.

A coral reef damaged by warmer ocean waters

PROTECTING NATURE

PRESERVATION

Although humans have caused a lot of damage to animal homes, many people are now trying to protect the health of fragile ecosystems. One way they are doing this is through preservation, or keeping wild places as natural and untouched as possible. Many places in the world have strict preservation rules.

Giant pandas became endangered in 1990. Since then, their natural habitats in China have been protected from deforestation and poachers. Thanks to preservation, the giant panda population has rebounded. Today, they are no longer considered endangered.

CONSERVATION

Conservation is slightly different from preservation. Conservation protects the environment from pollution and overdevelopment while still allowing humans to interact with nature in a **sustainable** way. People work to protect nature and take less from it.

New trees can be planted after others have been cut down. This keeps forests healthier for animals.

Large parts of the Amazon Rainforest have been burned and cut down to clear land for farms. New forms of sustainable farming reuse cleared land so less of the rainforest needs to be cut down. This protects the habitats of many animals.

HABITAT RESTORATION

Although many animal habitats have been destroyed by humans, there are some people who are now working hard to **restore** them.

MOUNTAIN GORILLA

Mountain gorillas live in the forests near central Africa's volcanoes. Their habitats have been damaged by farming, mining, and deforestation.

Mountain gorilla

In the 1980s, there were only a few hundred mountain gorillas left. Experts thought they would be extinct by the year 2000. Thanks to conservation efforts, there are now more than 1,000 mountain gorillas living in the wild.

SAIGA ANTELOPE

Saiga antelope almost disappeared from Earth due to hunting and habitat loss. In 2006, there were fewer than 50,000 left. Massive stretches of land in the country of Kazakhstan were restored to create more space for them. Thanks to this effort, there are now about a million saiga antelope in the wild.

Saiga antelope

ANTIGUAN RACER

Antiguan racer

In the 1890s, humans brought mongooses to the island country of Antigua and Barbuda to hunt rats. However, the small predators also hunted Antiguan racers, rare snakes found on the islands. By 1995, there were only 50 racers left. Thanks to restoration, their numbers are rising again.

REINTRODUCTION OF WILDLIFE

Sometimes, certain animals completely disappear from an area. Experts have found ways to **reintroduce** these animals to the places where they used to live.

Red Kites were reintroduced to the United Kingdom in the 1990s.

Animal species can be reintroduced in different ways. Sometimes, animals can be brought from a different location to replace the ones that have disappeared. Other times, scientists take a few animals into captivity. Once they have enough babies, the larger group can be moved back to their old home.

Wild horses were reintroduced to China in 1985.

TASMANIAN DEVIL

Tasmanian devils are small, furry creatures that used to live in forests across Australia. Due to disease, they began to disappear from the main part of the country and soon were only found on the island of Tasmania. In 2011, experts started to raise a population of the devils in captivity to prepare to reintroduce them to mainland Australia.

Tasmanian devil

In 2020, scientists released 26 Tasmanian devils into an Australian wildlife park. The scientists will observe and track the animals for several years to be sure they adjust to their new home.

WHO CAN HELP?

Lots of people around the world are doing their best to help animals. There are many different ways to get involved to help protect animals and their ecosystems.

Conservation specialists study the animals that are in danger and find out exactly what they need to survive. The scientists then work to provide as much protection as possible.

A scientist testing water for pollution

People are needed to help keep animals and their habitats safe. Rangers make sure parks are looked after and the animals who live there are not being harmed.

Researchers monitor ecosystems to make sure they are staying clean and healthy.

It is not only trained experts who protect animals. Many conservation groups get help from volunteer workers who do all sorts of jobs to improve the lives of animals. Even something as simple as picking up trash goes a long way to make animals and their homes safer and healthier.

WHAT YOU CAN DO AT HOME

You do not need to go deep into a jungle to help animals threatened by human activity. Wherever you live, you can do your part.

WILDFLOWERS

Planting wildflowers near your home can support lots of wildlife. Wildflowers that naturally grow where you live can provide food and shelter for bees, butterflies, and other insects. Even a small pot of wildflowers helps!

WOODPILES

Many bugs and small creatures make their homes in dark places. By stacking up dead wood, you can provide a place for bugs, such as beetles and spiders, to find food and raise their young.

FEEDERS

Putting up bird feeders is an easy way to help animals in your yard. You can make your own or get one from a store. Feeders can be especially helpful during times when it is difficult for birds to find food elsewhere, such as during a long winter.

29

HELPING ANIMALS

Although humans have done a great deal of damage to the animal kingdom, there is a lot we can do to make things right. Only humans have the power to reverse the damage they have done.

Helping wildlife is good for both people and animals.

Even helping just one animal can improve the ecosystem it is a part of. By respecting, caring for, and cleaning up the nature around you, you can do your part!

GLOSSARY

captivity a human-contained space where animals do not naturally live

chemicals substances, usually made by humans

climate the usual, expected weather in a certain place

deforestation the cutting down and clearing of forests

ecosystems interconnected communities of plants and animals

extinct when an animal has died out completely

fossil fuels fuels, such as coal, oil, and gas, that are made from the remains of plants that died millions of years ago

habitats places where plants and animals live or grow

migrate to move from one place to another during a certain time of year

population the total number of a kind of animal living in a place

predators animals that hunt other animals for food

reintroduce to bring an animal back into an area

restore to return something to its original form

species groups that animals and plants are divided into, according to similar characteristics

sustainable using without destroying or damaging future supplies or availability

toxic poisonous

INDEX

READ MORE

Bergin, Raymond. *Animals in Danger (What on Earth? Climate Change Explained).* Minneapolis: Bearport Publishing Company, 2022.

Feldstein, Stephanie. *Save Birds (Take Action: Save Life on Earth).* Ann Arbor, MI: Cherry Lake Publishing, 2024.

Walker, Tracy Sue. *Saving Endangered Species (Searchlight Books—Saving Animals with Science).* Minneapolis: Lerner Publications, 2024.

LEARN MORE ONLINE

1. Go to **www.factsurfer.com** or scan the QR code below.

2. Enter "**Wild Animals**" into the search box.

3. Click on the cover of this book to see a list of websites.